Contents

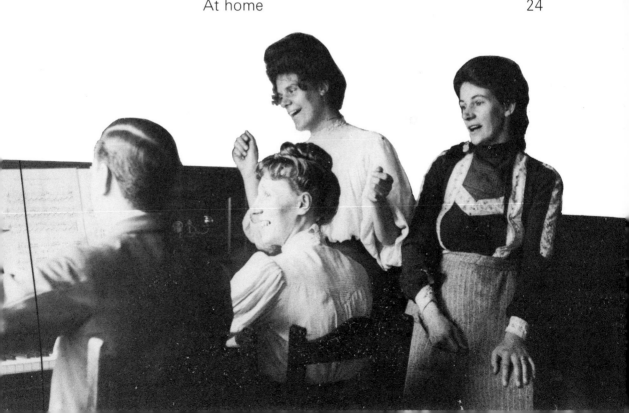

Outside the home

Wild Street, Heywood, Greater Manchester

Look at this old photograph. The children all lived in this street.
The houses are called terraced houses, or cottages.
Each one is joined to the house next door.

Look for:

— the windows called sash windows.
  You pushed them up to open them.
— the front doorsteps right on the pavement
— the street lamps, lit by gas
— the clothes the people are wearing.

**"We had no garden. All our mats had to be shaken outside
every morning before anybody was about."**

This family is standing outside the home. Find the sash window. Mother and father are dressed in their working clothes. The two children are wearing cotton pinafores over their dresses to keep them clean.

"We used to hang the washing on a line across the street."

___

Things to do

Start to make a book about life *At home in 1900.* If you can, find a street near where you live with terraced houses and no front gardens. Look for a house with sash windows. Draw a picture or take a photograph of it. Stick the picture in your book. Write about the houses and the street.

3

The family

There were five children in this family. They are wearing their best clothes in this photograph. Mother and the two girls have long dresses with full sleeves. Their lace collars are high up on their necks. The dresses are a tight fit.

"Girls wore a vest-bodice, drawers, three petticoats and a dark dress."

The Lockett family, Manchester

"In our day, our clothes had to be handed down. I was the youngest one and I used to get all the old clothes."

Father and the three boys are all wearing suits. Their jackets are buttoned tightly. The two older boys are wearing stiff collars. The younger boy, on the right, is wearing an open collar called a "sailor collar". Families in 1900, like this one, were larger than most families today.

"Very few people had more than two bedrooms. Five of us slept in the front bedroom. It had two double beds in it and a very big cot."

Things to do

Talk to someone older than 70.
Ask about their family:
— how many children were there in the family?
— what were their names?
— how many bedrooms did they have in their house?
Perhaps they can show you some old family photographs.

Draw some pictures and write about the clothes the people in the photographs are wearing.
Would you have liked wearing them?

"Out the back"

"The tap was outside and the lavatory was down the garden. There was no water with the lavatory. We used to take a pail of water with us."

St. John's Chapel, County Durham 1910

These two boys are sitting on their back doorstep.
One of them is writing on a slate.
You can just see inside the kitchen of the house.

Notice:

— the stone floor in the kitchen
— the broom for sweeping the kitchen floor.

In most people's homes there was only a cold water tap.
Sometimes it was in the kitchen. Sometimes it was outside.

The kitchen jars
and bowls were made
of earthenware.
Plastic had
not been invented.

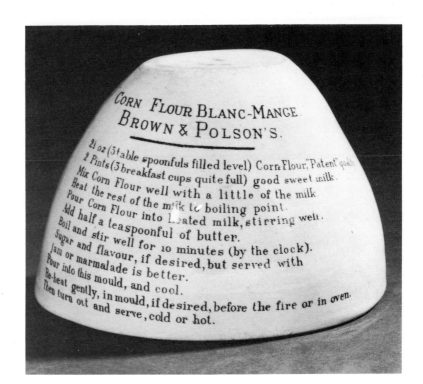

CORN FLOUR BLANC-MANGE.
BROWN & POLSON'S.

2½ oz (5 table spoonfuls filled level) Corn Flour "Patent" quality
2 Pints (3 breakfast cups quite full) good sweet milk.
Mix Corn Flour well with a little of the milk.
Heat the rest of the milk to boiling point.
Pour Corn Flour into heated milk, stirring well.
Add half a teaspoonful of butter.
Boil and stir well for 10 minutes (by the clock).
Sugar and flavour, if desired, but served with
Jam or marmalade is better.
Pour into this mould, and cool.
Re-heat gently, in mould, if desired, before the fire or in oven.
Then turn out and serve, cold or hot.

Things to do

Talk to an old person you know about the house
they lived in when they were your age.

Find out:

— if the tap was inside or outside?
— if they had hot and cold water taps?

In your book, write about the kitchen
and the water supply in 1900. Make a list of
all the things we need hot water for.

The kitchen

In every kitchen there was a fire like this one. It was called the kitchen range and was made of cast iron. Coal, wood and household rubbish were burnt on the fire. The kitchen was always warm.

"All the cooking was done on the kitchen range. We had big iron pans and kettles which got very black."

Look carefully at the photograph.

Find:

— the fire irons in front of the fire, left. These were used to put more coal on the fire and to poke out the old ash.
— the tray underneath the fire. The burnt ash fell into the tray. You could pull it out and throw the ash away.
— the oven on the left of the fire
— a saucepan, a kettle and an iron.

Every week the range was cleaned with
a special black polish called "black lead".

Food cooked on the range was simple.
Here are some old recipes:

**"Mother used to get three pennyworth of
beef and one pennyworth of liver.
She'd put it in the oven with some gravy."**

**"We used to take the top of a loaf,
put the kettle on and let the kettle steam
through it and make it nice and soft.
Then we'd put on some dripping,
pepper and salt. It was delicious.
We called it kettle broth."**

Things to do

Draw a picture of the kitchen range.

Ask someone old you know what food they liked
when they were your age.

Write the recipes in your book.

Keeping clean

"We had no bathroom in our house. In the corner of the bedroom was a washstand with a jug and basin."

Look at the photograph of a washstand.

Find:

— the jug standing in the basin.
   Water was carried upstairs in this big jug.
— the dish with a lid. The soap was kept in it.
— the jar, on the left. You put your toothbrush in this.
— the top of the washstand, on which the jug and basin
   are standing. This is made of stone called marble.
— the shiny tiles at the back, in case the water
   splashed when it was poured into the bowl.

Some old furniture shops still sell washstands like this one.

"When we wanted a bath, we had one in a zinc bath in front of the kitchen range."

"Sometimes we put a clothes horse round the bath, to keep a bit warmer.
We called the clothes horse a winter hedge."

"While we had our bath the jacket potatoes were cooking in the oven part of the range.
We ate them when we were dry."

Alfred, a Durham miner, 1913

Things to do

Write about *Bath night in 1900*.
Visit some shops which sell old furniture.

Look for:

— a washstand
— a jug and basin
— an old zinc bath.
Draw some pictures of them.

Lighting the home

There was no electric light in homes 80 years ago.

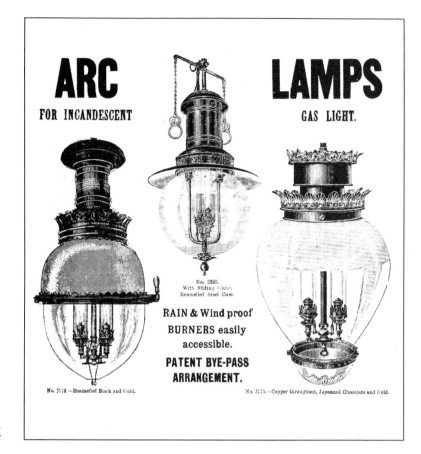

Right:
1899 advertisement

''Downstairs was lit by gas, with a gas mantle.
You had to be careful of the gas mantle.
It could easily get broken. You had to light
it half way first, so that it just glowed,
Then you had to put it full on.''

The gas came into the house in a metal pipe.
They had to pull a chain on the gas light
to switch the gas on. They lit it with a match.

"There were no lights upstairs. When we went to bed, we had to carry a lighted candle."

Things to do

In your book, write about *Lighting the home in 1900.*

Draw a picture of someone going up to bed carrying a candle.

If you can, find a poem by R. L. Stevenson called *Shadow March.*
It is about the strange shadows made by a flickering candle.

Baking bread

"We often baked our own bread. We spent one day a week baking. A man used to come round with yeast in a basket."

Do you know
what yeast is?
Why do we need
it to make bread?

The women in the
photograph are
baking bread in
an outside oven.
Everyone took their
bread there to be
baked.
Look at the crusty
loaves on the ground.
The woman on the right
is putting another
loaf into the oven.

You could also buy bread from
the baker. In the picture below you can
see his basket on top of the cart.

Look carefully at the cart.

Things to do

Find out how bread is made.
Write down what you find, in your book.

Make a list of all the things
you need to make bread.

Washday

"Monday was a busy day. We got up early, filled the copper with rainwater and lit a fire under the copper."

The copper had bricks around it. There was room inside for plenty of water, but it took a long time to heat up. When the water was hot, they took some out with a bucket. They poured the hot water into the washtub.

"We put dirty clothes in the tub of hot water and scrubbed them on a wash board. Sheets and towels were put in the dolly tub and were swished round with the poss stick."

Look for the woman turning the poss stick in the dolly tub.

The poss stick
is made of wood.
It is on the left
in this picture.
There is a washboard
on top of the dolly tub.

Things to do

How is your washing done?
How is the water heated?
Where are the sheets washed?

In your book, make two lists.
Call one list *Washday now*.
Write about doing the washing in your home.
Call the other list *Washday then*.
Write about doing the washing 80 years ago.

Ask an old person you know what they used
for washing before soap powder was made.

Left:
Dora and Hannah Blenkinsop,
St. John's Chapel, County Durham

"Any old iron!"

"After rinsing, the clothes were put through a mangle to squeeze out the water."

Made by Barker and Whitfield, Darlington

Here is a photograph of an old mangle. It is made of cast iron and wood. Can you see the handle on the wheel at the side?

The wheel made the heavy rollers turn. The wet sheets went through the rollers and the water fell into the box under the mangle. The other handle opened the wooden box. Then the sheets were hung outside to dry.

"For the ironing, flat irons were heated on top of the kitchen range."

Most people had 2 flat irons. While they used one, the other one was heating up on the kitchen range.

Four of the irons in the picture are flat irons. A block of metal was heated in the fire and then put into the space at the bottom of the iron. All the irons were very heavy.

Things to do

Which machine takes water out of washing today?
What heats the iron today?

Draw some pictures about washday 80 years ago.
Include heating the water, scrubbing the washing,
doing the mangling and the ironing.

Ask someone old you know what they can remember about washday.
Try to find someone who has an old flat iron.

Rugs

"The floors were covered with linoleum. To clean the house, we swept through it with a soft broom. Then the floors were washed with hot, soapy water."

Some people had carpets.

"We put old tea leaves on the carpet to lay the dust. Then we swept it with a stiff brush."

There was no electricity in the home in 1900, so there were no vacuum cleaners.

Most people knew how to make rugs for the floor.

"We used to wash our old clothes, cut them into pieces and push the pieces through an old piece of sacking with a brodder. A brodder was a piece of stick with a point at the end, like a pencil."

**"On fine days,
rugs were taken
outside and
beaten with
a carpet beater to
get the dirt out."**

Look at the picture.

Find:

— the carpet beater
— the pieces of material about
   1cm wide and 6cm long
— the large rag rug. Sometimes these rugs were
   called hooky rugs or peg rugs.

Things to do

Draw a picture of the inside of a living room.

Perhaps you can talk to someone who knows
how to make rag rugs. Try to make a small
rag rug of your own. You could use a knitting
needle as a brodder.

Amusements

There was no television in 1900. On winter evenings,
children played games and mothers and fathers did jobs in the house.

**"We played snakes and ladders, ludo and cards.
We did French knitting on a cotton reel."**

Some families were lucky enough to have a piano.

"That's how we enjoyed ourselves, singing round the piano. We had seven or eight in on a Sunday night, up to about midnight, playing and singing."

Here is a popular song they used to sing:

> "Daisy, Daisy, give me your answer, do.
> I'm half crazy, all for the love of you.
> It won't be a stylish marriage,
> I can't afford a carriage,
> But you'll look sweet upon the seat
> Of a bicycle made for two."

Things to do

Try to find out about other popular songs from 80 years ago. Perhaps you can make a recording of your grandparents or other elderly people singing some popular songs.

Draw a picture and write about the family singing round the piano.

At home

Mr. and Mrs. J. Gardiner, Rookhope, Weardale, County Durham

This photograph shows an elderly couple and their grand-daughter
seated beside the cooking range.

Look for the large pot and the kettle.

The little girl moved when the photographer took the picture.

Would you have liked to live in a home like this one in 1900?

The following museums have room interiors as part of their display:

The Geffrye Museum, Kingsland Road,
    Shoreditch, London
North of England Open Air Museum,
    Beamish Hall, Stanley, County Durham
Staffordshire County Museum,
    Shugborough, near Stafford
Museum of Oxford, St. Aldates, Oxford

Museum of East Anglian Life, Stowmarket,
    Suffolk
Nidderdale Museum, Council Offices,
    Pateley Bridge, North Yorkshire
Cookworthy Museum, Old Grammar School,
    Fore Street, Kingsbridge, Devon.
